CATS CATS CATS

CATS CATS CATS

A catalogue of cat cartoons

edited by S. Gross

COLUMBUS BOOKS
LONDON

Some of the cartoons in this collection have appeared in the following periodicals and are reprinted by permission of the authors: *Audubon, Better Homes and Gardens, Boys' Life, Campus Life, Cavalier, Cosmopolitan, Diversion, Family Circle, Good Housekeeping, Gourmet, House & Garden, Ladies' Home Journal, National Enquirer, National Lampoon, 1000 Jokes, Oui, Parade, Penthouse, Philadelphia Inquirer Magazine, Playboy, Punch, Saturday Evening Post, Saturday Review, This Week, TV Guide, Vision, Woman's Day, The Yacht.*

Grateful acknowledgment is made for permission to reprint:

Cartoons by Roz Chast from *Parallel Universes*. Copyright © 1984 by Roz Chast. Reproduced by permission of the author.
Cartoons by Henry Martin on page 98 from *Punch*. Copyright © 1979, 1983 by *Punch*. Reprinted by permission of Rothco Cartoons Inc. and the author.
Cartoons by John S. P. Walker. Reprinted from *Bad Dogs* by John S. P. Walker. Copyright © 1982 by John S. P. Walker. Reprinted by permission of Alfred A. Knopf. Inc. and Methuen and Company, Ltd.
Cartoons by Gahan Wilson on page 78 from *Playboy*. Copyright © 1972 by Playboy. Reproduced by special permission of *Playboy* magazine.
Cartoons copyrighted by *The New Yorker* are indicated throughout the book.

First published in Great Britain in 1987 by
Columbus Books Limited
19-23 Ludgate Hill, London EC4M 7PD

Reprinted 1987

Designer: Kim Llewellyn

Printed and bound in Great Britain by
The Guernsey Press Co. Ltd., Guernsey, Channel Islands.

ISBN 0 86287 367 3

"There's a silly sign if
I ever saw one."

BEWARE
OF
THE CAT

"Her landlord kicked her cat!
How did this thing ever get out of Small Claims Court?"

EVERETT OP

© 1967 The New Yorker Magazine, In

7

"Now, don't start complaining till you taste it."

REX MAY (BALOO)

THE CRAZY HOUR

Face gets wild.

Back hunches up ("Halloween kitty")

Noisy runs after invisible things.

GALUMPH
GALUMPH

Back to normal.

ROZ CHAST

9

"Could you show me something just a little more scratch-resistant?"

TIM HAGGERTY

O'NEILL   CATHARINE O'NEILL

"Hmm . . . looks like the bottom's falling out of the cat book market!"

"Does that include cats?"

SAM GROSS

"Now we've only two more kittens to unload."

"She has your eyes."

BERNARD SCHOENBAUM

"We have an important visitor today: the King of the Cats."

ED FISHER

CATHERINE SIRACUSA

"I hope you don't mind cat hairs."

FELIPE GALINDO (FEGGO)

THE AMAZING ADVENTURES OF BOB THE CAT AFTER HE WAS PUT TO SLEEP

"I think we'll take it, subject to his approval."

ED FRASCINO

MORT GERBERG

"Have you been made to feel welcome?"

23

"Don't forget to give Gertrude her pill."

DON OREHEK

Q: WHAT KIND of CATS ARE MOST FRIENDLY?

A: THOSE WHO HAVE THE WORST BREATH.

BERNARD SCHOENBAUM

"Peasant!"

HENRY MARTIN

"Our only consolation is that in about eleven years the controlling stockholder will be dead."

27

1. 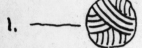 _____

2. _____  _____

3. _____  _____ _____

AARON BACALL *A. BACALL*

"You're purring. I like that in a cat."

JOHN CALLAHAN

S.GROSS

SAM GROSS

VAHAN SHIRVANIAN

"This is a solo number, if you don't mind."

LEE LORENZ

"We've been living together for six years, toots. How about getting hitched?"

ORLANDO BUSINO

"Did you get a description of the cat?"

THE VIGIL

1

2

3

4

5

6

7

8

(continued)

35

9

10

11

12

ANTHONY TABER
© 1977 The New Yorker Magazine, Inc.

ED FRASCINO

"I like dogs better. Dogs kiss."

37

PC VEY

P.C. VEY

"Have you ever read the label on a can of cat food? It reads 'all beef and beef byproducts.' . . .
Now tell me, do we look like either beef or beef byproducts?"

"You might as well introduce him to the 'treats' you got last year."

ANDY WYATT

BOOTH

GEORGE BOOTH
© 1975 The New Yorker Magazine, Inc.

"I *do* apologize, Rinehart. The cat has never bitten anyone previously."

"The Graysons are on vacation in Europe. I'm the sitter."

BARNEY TOH

SIDNEY HARRIS

"It's 20 cents a pound cheaper. *That's* why!"

Levin

ARNIE LEVIN

© 1977 The New Yorker Magazine, Inc.

"The artist was one of the first to experiment with the use of velvet
as an alternative to canvas."

BILL WOODMAN

CAT
BRAIN TEASER

1. Who is your owner?

A.  B.  C.  D.

2. Which of the following is inedible?

A.   B.  C.   D.

3. Name the scratchpost.

A.

B.

C.

D.

4. What happened to your little mouse-toy?

A.

Under couch

B.

Behind bookcase

C.

Turned into a ghost

D.

I don't know and
what's the difference?

WILLIAM HOES

"Actually it's turned out to be more of a cat feeder."

". . . and that's why a cat on a boat is considered bad luck."

BILL MAUL

"He's a confirmed bachelor."

ED FRASCINO

"No more Kitty-bits, Jenny. We're all Seventh Day Adventists now."

CATHARINE O'NEILL

"What's there to discuss?"

MICHAEL MASLIN

DON OREHEK

"Who do you think you're staring at!"

"Honey, I think the cat wants out!"

WALTER GALLUP

BERNARD SCHOENBAUM

"He's never been sick a day in his life except for an occasional fur ball."

"*Now* you tell me you get airsick!"

SAM GROSS

FELIPE GALINDO (FEGGO)

"He's merely putting the cat out, but he makes such a drama out of doing it."

ALEX NOEL WATSON

LITTLE KNOWN FACTS: A CAT WEIGHS TWICE

AS MUCH WHEN IT IS SLEEPING!

OLIVER CHRISTIANSON (REVILO)

TIM HAGGERTY

"Did you know you could throw out your back doing that?"

Anthony

ANTHONY TABER

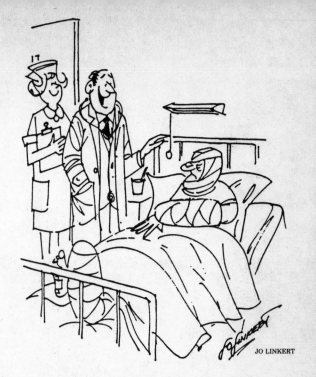

JO LINKERT

"Good news, Mr. Smith! The cat
got down safely."

"Meow! Pass it on!"

BORIS DRUCKER

BOOTH

GEORGE BOOTH

"He sure fooled me . . . I didn't think he gave a damn about anything."

THOMAS CHENEY

"When you told me you were an ailurophile I thought you were into some kind of kinky sex."

ED FRASCINO

"Jonathan!"

DON OREHEK

65

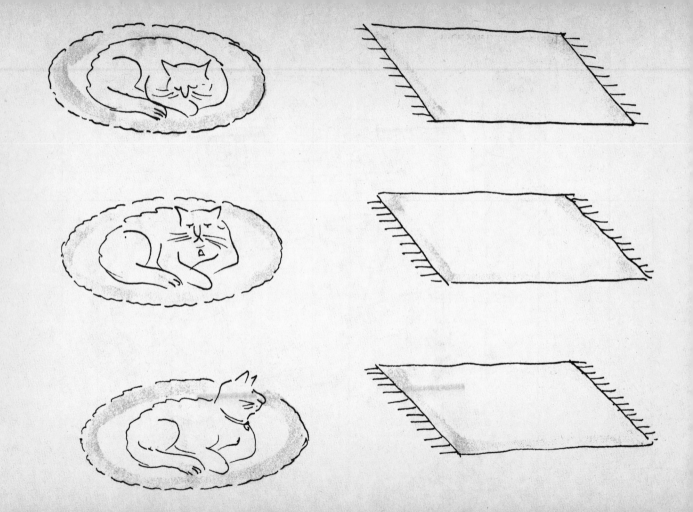

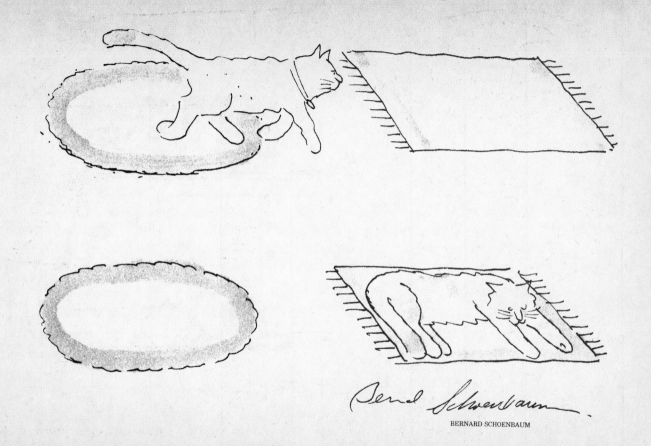

BERNARD SCHOENBAUM

VAHAN SHIRVANIAN

68

HENRY MARTIN

"I wrote a letter to the president of the company about the red food dye in your Turkey and Chicken Parts and he wrote back a two-page letter, the bottom line of which was something about consumerism, test marketing, and finicky eaters."

MORT GERBERG

"You wouldn't be purring so smugly if you knew we were careening into poverty."

"Look, I already have a cat clock, a cat calendar, cat cushions, and a cat lamp—so beat it."

MICHAEL MASLIN

THE PUSSYCAT OLYMPICS

MICK STEVENS

SAM GROSS

"According to the note, they voted 8 to 3
to come live with their father."

"What is it with you, anyway?"

FRANK MODELL

MAUL

"Sit up!"

"Lie down!"

"Heel!"

"Give a paw!"

"Roll over!"

CATHARINE O'NEILL C'NEILL

"Congratulations, Mr. Stevens. Sally graduat*
summa cum laude from the Canby Cat
Obedience School."

74

"I know it's not Perrier, but that's all that's available."

PETER PORGES

75

"Darn! We forgot the non-temperamental cats!"

MICHAEL CRAWFORD

"Cat out?"

"Here, puss, puss, puss!"

FELIPE GALINDO (FEGGO)

ARNIE LEVIN
© 1975 The New Yorker Magazine, Inc.

ED FRASCINO

"I haven't been happy, but I pretend for her sake."

VAHAN SHIRVANIAN

"Two martinis, very dry, one with an olive, one with a goldfish."

TIM HAGGERTY

JETÉ

Bernard Schoenbaum

BERNARD SCHOENBAUM

"City mouse, country mouse—
I'm not particular."

CHARLES SAUERS

"First the good news—kitty finally came home. . . ."

ORLANDO BUSINO

"Bank robbery, safe cracking, counterfeiting, forgery, no, no, no . . . you had to become a cat burglar!"

THOMAS CHENEY

STUART LEEDS

85

"Pegler drank a toast to Mrs. Pegler, then he drank a toast to each of Mrs. Pegler's thirteen cats. That's too damn many cats!"

GEORGE BOOTH

THE FOUR CAT BREEDS

Domestic Pettables

Complete Paranoids

These cats can take as much affection as you're willing to dish out. This includes hugging by 2-year-olds. They can be found anywhere and everywhere. Look for the tell-tale "I aim to please" expression and congenital bow.

These felines are rarely seen except under furniture and in the back of closets. You might have one and not even know it.

Foreign Costabundles

$6,000.00

True Costabundles are recognized by their subliminal pricetags and nitwit owners. They tend to do a lot of sleeping

Stranges

This unfortunate group appears mainly in cat shows and in the imaginations of people who think of themselves as "cat fanciers." Hairlessness, wrinkly skin, rat-tails, and weird facial expressions are a few of their attributes.

R. Chast
ROZ CHAST

TODAY IS THE FIRST DAY OF THE REST OF YOUR NINE LIVES

A. BACALL

AARON BACALL

JOHN CASSADY

"Just because he's been declawed—
don't think he's any less dangerous."

"She can't understand it. You're not shedding and she is."

ORLIN
RICHARD ORLIN

"I'll tell you one thing, Percy, there aren't many cats like you."

BILL WOODMAN

"Edgar, please run down to the shopping center right away, and get some milk and cat food. Don't get canned tuna, or chicken, or liver, or any of those awful combinations. Shop around and get a surprise. The pussies like surprises."

"You're getting fat, Jason, too fat to do anything."

BORIS DRUCKER

"Of course she's beautiful. She sleeps eighteen hours a day."

ED FRASCINO

BERNARD SCHOENBAUM

"That's nothing. You should have been here five minutes ago when the dish ran away with the spoon."

HENRY MARTIN

"I tell you, the book has everything—sex, history, consciousness, and cats!"

WILLIAM HAMILTON

COMPLAINTS

S. GROSS

SAM GROSS

1

2

3

4

5

6

VAHAN SHIRVANIA

"Well, I hope you're proud of yourself!"

MISCHA RICHTER
© 1979 The New Yorker Magazine, Inc.

"We have fourteen cats, but Kevin thinks we only have twelve."

"Boots is getting too fat to sleep on the car!"

DON OREHEK

"There, it's down! Now give her nine of these pills daily."

ORLANDO BUSINO

"Cats are *so* independent!"

"Pounce!"

CHARLES SAUERS

"Your cat is entering my sphere of influence!"

BORIS DRUCKER

THE
Evolution
of
Catfish

JOHN S.P. WALKER

ED FRASCINO

"I think he realizes what a lucky kitty he is."

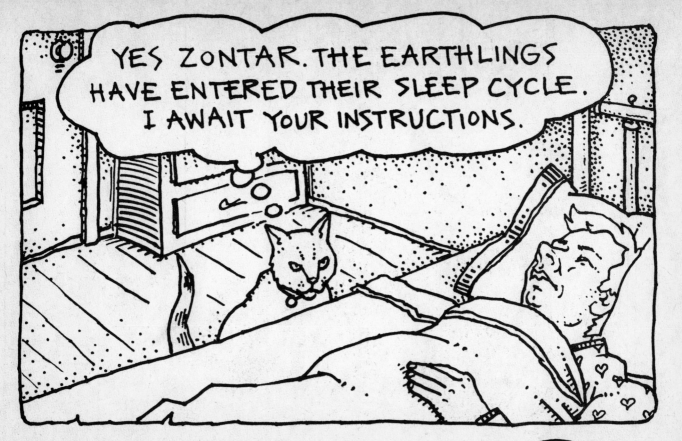

OLIVER CHRISTIANSON (REVILO)

"I used to have lots of little pussycats, but I decided it was easier
to have one great big pussycat."

LEE LO

WOODMAN

BILL WOODMAN

AARON BACALL

"That's a sacrilege!"

ANDY WYATT

"He really needs a bath but the tab on his collar says to dry clean only."

114

"We found her hiding in one of the closets."

SAM GROSS

1

2

3

4

BERNARD SCHOENBA

JERRY MARCUS *Jerry Marcus*

"It seems the only thing you remembered to do around here was to put the cat out!"

"Yes, my darling—I *know* that Chessy is crying out for you—and so am *I*!"

MORT GERBERG

"You're going to have a nice long life and have lots of kittens. Now scat!"

BORIS DRUCKER

ARNOLDO FRANCHIONI

"They're Siamese cats."

J.J. SEM

"I didn't mind it so much before Flossy had kittens."

JOHN JONIK

MICHAEL MASLIN

Something the Cat Dragged In

BUD GRACE

"It's not that I don't trust you, Estelle, but before I eat this oatmeal
I want to see the box that it came in."

BERNARD SCHOENBAUM

"My! Aren't we bright-eyed and bushy-tailed this morning."

O'NEILL

CATHARINE O'NEILL

"At first it was the occasional bit of tunafish and, I don't know, one thing just
led to another."

1

2

3

4

CALLAHAN

127

"Cats—you can't live with them, and you can't live without them."

LEO CULLUM